DISCOVER SERIES
BEACH

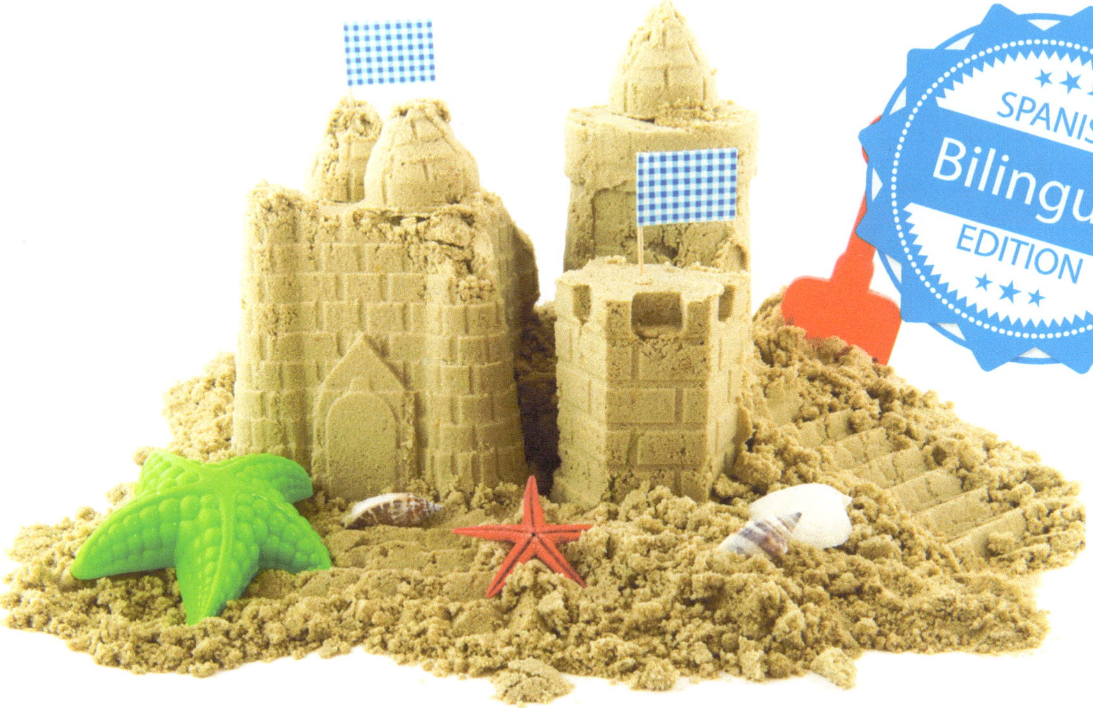

SPANISH
Bilingual
EDITION

PLAYA

Pelota de Playa

Beach Ball

Cubeta de Playa

Beach Bucket

Silla de Playa

Beach Chair

Playa Cerrada

Beach Closed

Bicicleta Crucero

Beach Cruiser

Piedras de Playa

Beach Rocks

Toallas de Playa

Beach Towels

Collar de Cuentas

Bead Necklace

Traje de Baño de Papá

Dad's Swim Trunks

Hamaca

Hammock

Salvavidas Juvenil

Junior Lifeguard

Anillo de la Vida

Life Ring

Máscara y Snorkel

Mask and Snorkel

Mensaje en la Botella

Message in a Bottle

Traje de Baño de la Mamá

Mom's Bathing Suit

Palmera

Palm Tree

Castillo de Arena

Sand Castle

Dolar de Arena

Sand Dollars

Colección de Conchas del Mar

Sea Shell Collection

Crema para el Sol

Sun Cream

Gafas de Sol

Sunglasses

Tablista

Surfer

Aletas de Natación

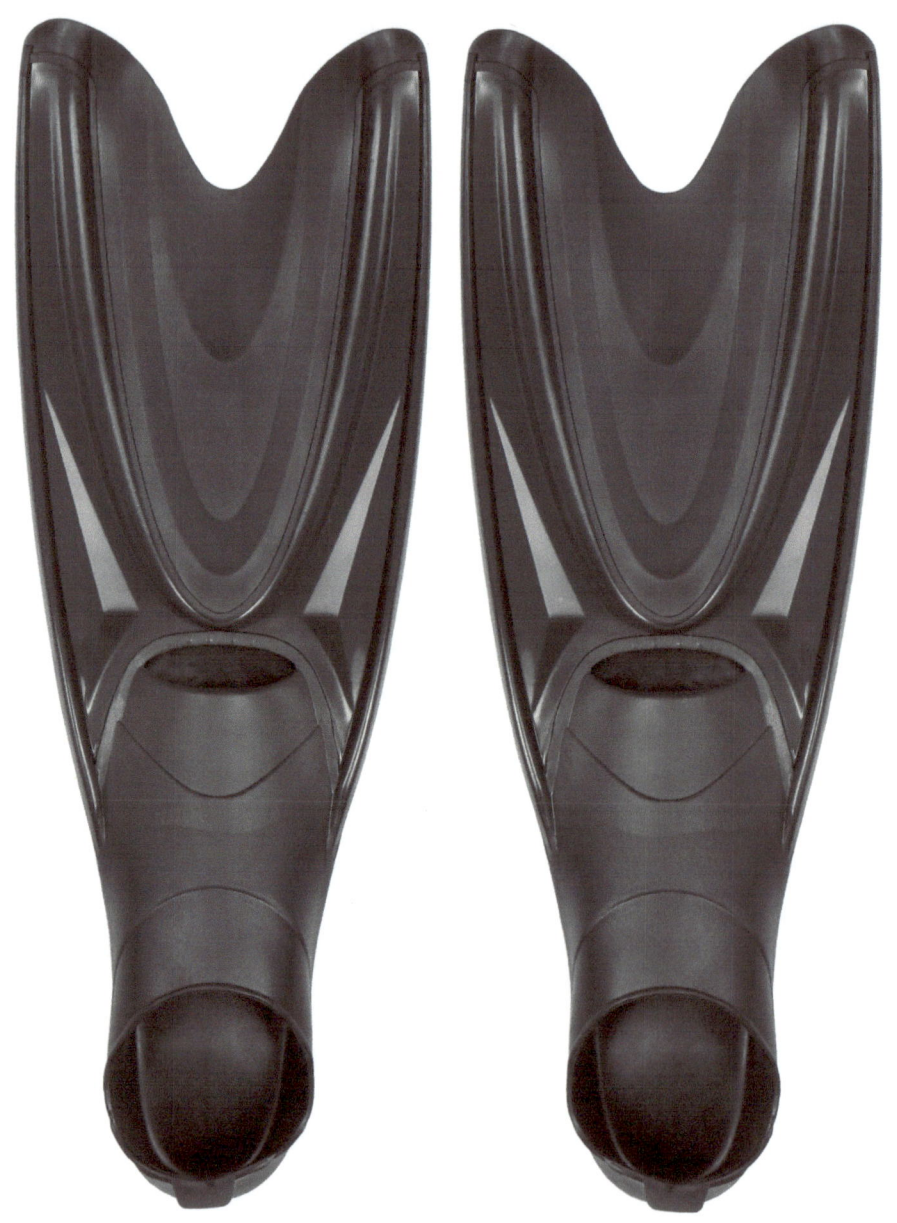

Swim Fins

Anillo de Natación

Swim Ring

Voleibol

Volleyball

Make Sure to Check Out the Other Discover Series Books from Xist Publishing:

Published in the United States by Xist Publishing
www.xistpublishing.com
PO Box 61593 Irvine, CA 92602

© 2017 First Bilingual Edition by Xist Publishing
Spanish Translation by Victor Santana
All rights reserved
No portion of this book may be reproduced without express permission of the publisher
All images licensed from Fotolia
ISBN: 978-1-53240-094-0 EISBN 978-1-53240-138-1

xist Publishing

www.ingramcontent.com/pod-product-compliance
Lightning Source LLC
LaVergne TN
LVHW071031070426
835507LV00002B/107

*9 781532 400940 *